The
Different Levels
of
Love

VOL. 2

The
Different Levels
of
Love

VOL. 2

DAVID WRIGHT

DIPS
Publishing

The Different Levels of Love, Volume 2

Published by DIP'S
Publishing Cleveland, OH
www.thinkforyourself.life

ISBN: 978-1-946818-12-6
Printed in the United States of America

I dedicate this to Marleen A Carabello, my muse and my best friend. You have always been there for me when I needed you and at times when I didn't. I love you isn't a strong enough expression because it leaves too much feeling out. I have written many things with you as my inspiration, I thank you for that. I will always be a friend to the one that was always honest with me, and there to listen. If I had to give a title to the bond that we share, it would be "For Life". I have known you for more than half of my life and all but 14 years of yours. Our friendship has grown from a sapling to a full grown Redwood. We will stand the test of time because what we have is real. You have been a counselor, a sister, and a most valued friend in my life. When we were young we often discussed our dreams and goals. It does not amaze me that we're achieving, because we dedicated our lives to family and success. This dedication is my way of saying thank you. Thank you for listening, thank you for loving and thank you for understanding; Me. You are and will always be; much appreciated!

CONTENTS

The Different Levels of Love

VOL. 2

It's been a pleasure

To have had you as a friend for all these years. I see brothers that can't claim the bond that we shared. You have been there for me more times than I can count. When family wasn't, you were; no matter what in my corner. I wasn't raised with you, but you treat me as if we climbed out of the same womb. Together even. At times treating me better that I have treated myself. It's been a pleasure, such a friend! Watching you now, yes I weep. But only joy am I experiencing, let your soaked arm remind all of what kind of man you were. The kind that could make the strong weep. A man's man, and ITS BEEN A PLEASURE TO CALL YOU FRIEND. An honor, some brag on possession, some brag on wealth but I here now brag on you. You are my brother, and I'm great full to have had a friend like you. I think of all the times that we've shared and my brother truly, ITS BEEN A PLEASURE!

Simply beautiful

Simply Beautiful you are without even trying. So blessed I am, in the Lords favor daily I find myself because you have never left me. I wake up and sometimes question my worthiness. Having you by my side makes me ask why. Why have I been chosen to receive such a gift? I know it isn't repayment for something I've done because I have done nothing so great to have received a payment like you. Simply beautiful you are, majestic even. Your movements exude such grace and harmony. I sometimes watch you as you sleep, in slumber your even a Queen. You breathe as if giving instruction to your royal court. Pleasantly portraying how simply beautiful you truly are; without even trying. Never a rash movement your spirit always in step. Whether sleep or awake, you are simply beautiful. Mesmerizing me with even your thought, the way you walk, talk and smile. Simply beautiful you are in every way, and I'm blessed that you are mine!

Beautiful moments

We share connecting in a tangled mesh of feelings ever so slowly growing closer. Exploring each other but are always respectful of boundaries set. While still having every intention of pushing beyond them. Not yet in love but it is a very deep like. On the brink of but not yet quit. Passion is not the only push behind us. We are best friends so moving closer is as natural as it gets. Beautiful moments being created sometimes by just sharing silence. Beautiful moments we share and I wouldn't change a thing about us. Our down's make our ups that more noticeable, that more appreciated. That more beautiful.

I know why I was lonely

I was lonely Because this was my time to stay focused. I have finally arrived at sight, I can finally see; clearly. I can see the me inside of me, it was a must that I stayed unattached. If only to keep myself ready, I know why I was lonely and I completely understand. I now get it, I now know that if I wasn't lonely I might have changed my mind. I might have focused on the them instead of the it. The it; that part of God in me that I now do let hold my attention. I have found all the friendship that I needed for then in the power of the way, the truth and the light. That being said, I know why I was lonely. But as we speak I'm understanding and drawing to me the end of my loneliness. I know why I was lonely, it's because I had a job to do before I met you!

You have my heart in a headlock

And I can't seem to get free. Your movements often don't reflect the way that I agree with life being; in my mind's eye seeing. But still I endure, because I love you. I mean honestly I can't think of any more honest of a way to express myself. I see the love I see in you but all I hear is words of friendship from you. Purposely I travel this road, however long and bumpy it's been. We live our existence daily in thought and I wonder what has brought me to such a limbo for such a length of time. As I ask, the question has been answered. Me! But you are formidable, an opponent worthy of the belt. You have my heart in a head lock, I struggle but am unable to break free of your grip. Sometimes I can't breathe, your headlock is that strong. Sometimes it resembles a choke hold. You have my heart in a head lock. Either fight fair or let me go.

I know you're doing your best

I look deep into your eyes Oh husband of mine and I know that you're doing your best. Your best might not be enough for some, but your best is more than enough for me. You are strong and I see that. I see your strength in every move you make and in every dollar you save. Careful to never let us fall by the waste side. I thank you for not giving up. I thank you for letting your old ways go and for putting your family first above all else. You are my man, and I love you. I have all the faith and confidence in the world in you. I know that everything will be ok. Because I know that you're doing your best.

Really

There is no more us, you REALLY mean this?

You mean that when I call you will no longer be there for me? I know I struggle in my ways but I REALLY can't stand the thought of losing you. You have been the strength in my shoulders for so long now. I know that I have a good women. Would you REALLY walk away? Even tho you know that I love you and you know that I care? If there is nothing I can do then there isn't. If my flaws disheartens your heart so much so that you would rather walk away. Then I won't attempt to stop you. I will only love you forever, yes I REALLY will!

I don't care about your past

In my mind you are brand new, your yesterday's are the past and they are long forgotten by me. My only concern is our tomorrow's and the beautiful days that lie ahead of us. I am not attempting to pretend that your scars and the thoughts of unpleasant situations you've been through in the past don't linger inside you and at times cause grief. I only say that whatever you have been through, it doesn't matter to me. You are able to be free from those mistakes or regrets. I want you to be able to be yourself with me. Let those unpleasant yesterdays you've experienced serve to teach; not to crumble your spirit. I don't care about your past, it is as unimportant as yesterday's news. Trash is discarded, and your past, to me has been as well. I seek to learn the new you, the new you that will emerge beyond this point of your past. Into a you that was only made possible because of it. And now For us, the past plays no part; there are only the roads towards the future and our happiness that awaits!

Like I do

You don't feel like I do, and that's fine. I am meant to learn from this I'm sure. Time is never wasted. Its benefits may be mistaken/ and possibly hidden but they are always there. To mentally be still and to notice them is the thing that must be done. I digress, You don't feel like I do, that doesn't make you wrong. It just makes me lonely, it just forces me to live outside of your love. I don't understand but the decisions we make are always ours. Right or wrong matters not because whatever the outcome—it is ours alone to love or hate, curse or praise. You not feeling like I do used to hurt but now it just boosts my faith. It makes me think; I am worthy of the greatest that life has to offer am I not! What is mine can't be denied me; correct! So if you aren't mine, you can't be the best thing for me! I deem you to be God's gift, the most he has to offer, that only means a bigger and greater gift from God for me awaits. I claim my destiny before it comes, so all who see can understand that the love that will soon materialize for me. I EXPECTED IT! You don't feel like I do, and that's ok. Because someone, one day… SOON…that's all I desire and more…WILL!

Doing my best

To be honest it doesn't get much realer than this; a man doing his best. Against all odds and adversities I compete and eventually triumph! Tired I am at the end of the day and weary I am at the start but I'm still doing my best. You may not understand why I'm not winning right now but for that perfect one, me doing my best will be good enough. It will actually be more than enough. She understands and recognizes a man doing his best when she sees one. She knows that there aren't an abundance of men like me out there. Men that know matter what do—their best. Most guys do their best while everyone's watching or when he knows that he will be rewarded or paid handsomely for the task at hand. But a man like me that's Doing My Best just because, just because my best is all I know and all that I have to give? Guys like me are extinct, or dying at a rapid rate while very few are being reproduced. Doing my best always separates me from the rest. I do what I need to do, I do what's expected of me and more! I'm Doing My Best!

Feel good

I feel good, about you, about me about us. I feel good about this world. I want to make my Feel Good feelings be felt by you, you and you. I want to be as a virus and infect others with this feeling. I pray that there be an epidemic. An epidemic of people coming down with feeling good. I promise to neglect this disease so it will spread. I will hug others and kiss all I can. With every touch my mentality the way that I FEEL, GOOD. You will too. I only want to make you sick, don't look at me so strange. When you become infected by this, you won't die. You will live! Begin to live in the state of mind that all is right not all is wrong. In the mind frame of I love myself and I love you to. In spite of you will I still be there. No matter what. I feel good, after hearing this...don't you feel good too?

Love each other

Let us let the spirit work through us for us and to all of our benefit. We have suffered long enough have we not. Giving away so much of ourselves as we continue loosing and wondering why. Loving each other will inspire higher thought. And higher thought will in turn inspire us to love each other. A grand dance with only the beat of our individual vibrations in the back round. Loving each other will set us free, free from the box opposite of love we have found ourselves in. We are weakened by any thought we have contrary to loving each other. Walking around helpless in hate when we could be made strong if we would simply Love Each Other!

You matter

You matter because you are you. You were created from stardust and shaped into the form of a God. You matter even if you are never told that you do. When your gone you are missed, and when present you are loved. I need you, you matter. Every thought that you have means something. Every thought helps to inspire another. You matter, in this way let the chain reaction you set in motion end with a blessing. The chain reaction induced by your thought. Let it be as great as water is to the world. You matter, bring those thoughts into this world and change it. You matter, you, your thoughts and everything you embody. This earth will slow down a step when your gone, so let us benefit while your here. You matter and we couldn't change the world without you.

Closer and closer

We move towards each other. With the ups and downs we face together and through everything we endure; on the other side of this struggle, we find strength. A strength that enables us to handle more of life—together. We are becoming one, a single circle, unbreakable. Closer and closer we grow, I give you the chance to express yourself. While You give me the opportunity to lead, a unit moving with precision. I am not here to evaluate you, only to love and to help you grow. As you grow, so do I—as I understand so does your level of faith increase. We need each other for nothing, because we both are more than capable. But our partnership allows us to do more, to be in two places at once. We are getting on the same page now; as we move, Closer and Closer.

Then along came you

And I knew that there was more to living than just myself. The day you came into my life, I forever gave up the notion of I. And could only utter the references to we when the idea presents itself. The moment after you entered my life, a new dedication emerged. My soul and spirit were reborn, I knew that from that moment on I was responsible and would have to answer to the creator; accountable for more than just myself. Then you came along, and all my wrongs seemed to finally equate to something other than just more wrongs. I have to say thank you to my creator for giving me the power to create! For I planted my seed and Then along came you!

Your beauty I still see

After all these years, as your smile has inevitably changed with age. Through the grey hairs and under the wrinkles after all this time, your beauty I still see. It doesn't make any difference to me how you've changed; your beauty has only evolved. You look just as lovely as the day we met. I close my eyes and can relive the best moment in my life like it was yesterday. You are a vision of loveliness and after all these years your beauty I still see. The spirit that inhabits your body, your way of sharing and caring; you make me fall in love again every day. You are my heart and through the years, through our difficulties through all of our ups and downs; Your Beauty I Still See!

As the years pass

I only fall deeper and deeper in love with you. I've learned not to judge but rather experience what others have to offer. Being able to take in what you give off has given to me a sense of completeness. It's strange that what you need most in your life can be facilitated by another. As the years pass I gain ground in becoming a newer me. But in you I'm able to grow because your insight polishes me. Your critiques of me make me better, as the years pass I have come to see your worth. Your exterior gains time but you age only in grace. The phrase "created in his image" addresses all that you are and as the years pass all that you have become. I adore you, the years by your side have seemed to pass in a blink. My only regret is that there isn't more time for me to love you. As the years pass I promise never to miss an opportunity to express how truly precious to me you are. I love you very much and as the years pass that love constantly grows!

Off my feet

You knock me off my feet, beauty stunning and character matching that of an angel. I know that I am blessed to have been chosen to receive a love such as yours. We move closer in connecting and understanding that which is separate at birth but joined together voluntarily in an attempt to become one. Our oneness is uniting us in a way that neither of us for saw. We both are able to recognize our level of us getting stronger and growing closer. Truly taking on a life of its own. Never could we have envisioned this level of commitment being created by the words "I do." You knock me off my feet, and I never want to stand again!

A piece of a woman

To have only a chip of the HOPE DIAMOND or ten percent of a billion dollar fortune would still make a man a baron would it not? I say that you are so beautiful inside and out THAT TO only have A piece of a woman like you would still make any man just as wealthy. Just a piece of a woman like you would no doubt be enough because your all might be overwhelming. Like Moses looked away as not to behold the full glory, I say that a piece of a woman like you would put to shame some others women's wholes! Your character is what it takes, "WHO CAN FIND A VIRTUOUS WOMAN, FOR HER PRICE IS FAR ABOVE RUBIES." Again just a piece of a woman like you for me would be enough.

Doing me/loving myself

Gently I coddle my spirit to get on the same page and to identify. I often take An outside view when looking at myself. That is why I have such a problem knowing me. I live inside as do we all, inside is a place where only the self and a trusted few know the real you. But inside isn't where we reside. We have a magnificent home inside ourselves but we live looking out of the window. Allowing what we see to dictate how we feel. We want this item or that object we saw instead of becoming that thing to create those things we admire. Thereby putting an end to need! Doing me/Loving myself is the discovery of what lies underneath all the superficial things we are. This is the real exploration, explanation and exhalation of what we could become. I'm about to start DOING ME/LOVING MYSELF!

It's time to let go

You are on another journey other than the one you and I had previously embarked on. Although its time To let go, it's hard. I feel a connection, I feel a bond between us. I must as tough as it is keep reminding myself however that you don't because if you did we wouldn't be having this conversation. We would be somewhere of loving each other, we would be living; together. But since we aren't, after all this time; it's time to let go. This experience has been like being stuck in the mud, or running a race with no Finish line. No matter how much effort is exerted; no matter how hard I try, I get nowhere and I can't win. Each instance amounts to a colossal waste of time and another way being needed. It's time to let go, I have let go before, maybe I should say that it's time to let go; AND NEVER LOOK BACK!

I just always thought we would be

It hurts to say goodbye, not because I can't in some way make it on my own. It hurts to say goodbye just because I always thought that we would be. In loosing you, I feel such anguish. It never crossed my mind us not being. I just always thought we would be! My tomorrows hold a future that will not obtain you. That seems strange, but it will have to be. Time heals all wounds, so one day this feeling will to develop a scab and become old. I choose to acknowledge the feeling, out of respect; it's better to have loved and lost than to never have loved at all. I'm growing better as I vent, the scar is already beginning to heal. I'm not sad any longer, you win some and lose the rest. I just always thought we would be!

Me and my baby

We must have been dipped in the same substance and created from the same mold, in unison our souls emerging out of creation; together. Dripping with stardust! Me and My baby, your being here lets me know that this is all real. Jesus is Love and that is all that I have for you. I am alive—yes—but I've not always felt this level of existence coursing through my veins. My baby has been the difference for me. Me and My baby, together conquering all that approaches not on the same accord. We notice your beauty and move as one as to take full advantage of what your nature has to offer. Two peas in a pod, me and my baby! May we last, let this love grow not die, always full of life and never withering! Me and My Baby, here for you and so we can be here for each other! Basking in the glow of the sunset and walking on the beach hand in hand, MENTALLY, in an amazing love story. Me and my baby!

You are the one

I hold you so close because I can't get enough of your presence. You are the one! For me there are no others, you are the one that my heart belongs too. I awake every morning to see if the dream I have been living all these years will be over and I will finally be forced to wake up. I am living a blissful reality, with my mental interpretation of fantasy; as a companion. How could this not be compared to a dream; heaven. If this feeling holds no comparison then the a for mentioned places could not possibly exist. You are the one that through him provides for me; a level of love that is cosmic and on a galactic scale. I have never prayed for wealth and riches because your supply is infinite. I only prayed to have someone to love FOREVER; and something tells me—YOU ARE THE ONE!

I'm through with Love

This is my last time caring, and devoting myself to one. I'm through with love. But let's stop for a moment and be clear—throwing in the towel in this case—in this instance isn't admitting defeat. Rather it is a calculated retreat. I say that I'm through with you only because Love, you have been through with me. Why cry over spilled milk, you weren't meant for me any way. If you were, the rest of that statement will have to fill in itself; I'm through with love. I remember a time when first starting out, Love; you meant so much. How refreshing your presence was. I couldn't wait to greet you in the morning. Always on my mind you were! Now all I do is try and forget, how at this time in my life I would welcome amnesia; I'm through with love. I have no regrets, I've just learned my lesson. I will now and forever love only myself. Wow, excuse me. Ma'am, you are quite beautiful, my name is David Wright Sr. Oh my God; I think I'm in love.

Tonight

Tonight will be our first time. Our first time becoming one; our first time making love. Under God and heaven; penetration unifies us. You are my last exploration, I will never need another after you. Tonight, I will make you an honest woman. Meaning that tonight I complete the story since a child you've been telling of finding the perfect man. Tonight I make your vision, your words flesh. For they have come full circle in the manifestation of me. Tonight I will bring you pleasure, such that you have never seen or known. My whole life has led me to this point, my whole life has played out in preparation for tonight! I will be gentle with you and your heart, it will be handled with great care in this lifetime and the next, because tonight we will now and forever become one!

Someone to love

I'm looking right now for someone to love, someone that is just for me. Someone that will accept me the same as I do them and share their lives. I'm so weary of one sided love. People expect but aren't interested in providing what they themselves want. Giving nothing but anticipating everything in return. Impossible to understand, but easily noticed. So alone I am, looking for Someone to Love. I'm not seeking perfection by any means, my standards are such that I'm flexible. I just want true love, true love from a well rounded women not afraid of being honest. A woman with morals that values my opinion; as I do hers. A woman that will trust me; trust me with her heart. A woman that is prepared to love back; no matter what she has been through! A woman that can talk, express and share her feelings with me, trusting that I will understand; any and everything she says. I want a woman that doesn't doubt and will cling to me above all others; even family. Am I now striving to find a super woman? No, I will accept you for you—no matter your faults! I just want someone true, I just want someone real that cares enough to try, I just want someone to love!

Breathing room

Give me some space please, you are suffocating me. Your love is out of control, all you see is what your eyes set themselves upon. Real or not, you pursue it. Much of the anguish you experience is brought upon yourself. You don't know when to stop, you over love. I need breathing room, a chance to miss you. A chance to reenergize my battery. I am so drained, fighting you of is exhausting. If only you would understand, love doesn't have to be so much pressure. It should be spontaneous, not planned. My frustration is slowly becoming anger, after is hate. I don't seek to leave you, I'm just crying out for a little breathing room!

Just for you

Just for you, I take the time out now to write this poem. It is Entitled Just for you. So special you are without even trying; like the sunshine on a Dank day. Your beauty at times is overwhelming, you are a masterpiece of perfection. Just for you I would do anything, travel to the ends of the earth to help to facilitate a smile on your face. You make me happy, So just for you to be comfortable and mentally at ease I everyday without question give my all. I work hard to provide, gladly. I am a man because I am a man but just for you I would face any danger head on. Just for you I would gladly walk into hell smack the devil and walk out. Just for you I provide my love and a stability that would not, could not be given to another; because it is Just for you.

How we were

When I loved you and you loved me. Back when we took the time to hear and were concerned with what the other said. In the beginning before love, misperceptions and suspicions got in the way. I'm talking about back when we trusted each other; when either of us could do no wrong. Once upon a time when we forgave and weren't so judge mental towards each other. How we were seems like an eternity to what we've become. We have no patience, no understanding. The harder one tries the more the other resists. Like hatred and distain have become the new face of love. At least in our world. I see us in my mind and I hold fast to this prayer. That we can find the magic and become once again; How We Were.

When they care enough

They are next to you, caring. Around to be there when you need them. When they care enough, you never have to look far for them. Even when they are miles away, they are close by. Love is auspicious, giving us the ability to do more than humanly possible when it's present. When they care enough, you never have to wonder. Steps taken carefully or not but all more than evidently in your direction. When they care enough your never confused, your more than confident in the ground you stand on being solid. When they care enough you feel safe, you feel able. When they care enough, you know it!

Thanks to you

Thanks to you, I am still here. Momma without your help I would have met my demise in the gutters of my ambitions a long time ago. But Thanks to you, Momma, I am still here. More loving, wiser and able to understand my gifts and to constructively apply them to the creative process. Thanks to you, I now am raising children of my own, with the same tough love you raised me with. Thanks to you, I am able to relate to my offspring in a manner conducive to their success. Thanks to you, I am able to lead by example and mold by experience. Thanks to you, I know what the word power really means. I know that in turning the other cheek you express the only true power that is powerful enough to deserve mention; control. Thanks to You, momma, I get it. I only can hope and pray that one day my children will be able to say, "Daddy, thanks to you."

Deep in your eyes

Deep in your eyes I look and I see myself, I see all that I want to become in you. My destiny is pre written meaning I'm laced with greatness but I know that with you by my side I will achieve; any and everything! You make me feel incredible, like I'm super human. A virtues and Godly woman is the power pack to any strong man. I know that you are my future and I claim it; your presence serves to validate my efforts. You would make a fitting Queen to any King. But deep in your eyes however I look and know that you are mine; and meant only for me. Deep in your eyes I look and know that my love is inside you, growing and developing—taking on a life of its own. Our spirits are joined because deep in your eyes is where I feel safe, is where I feel loved is where I feel home!

How much

How much I love you can't be put into words! Yes I have made terrible mistakes, but let them not go as the expression of my feelings! Instead of the wrongs committed being used to define my love, please let the sunrise that comes up daily blessing us with warmth and light be the mascot for me. If not that, then use the rain that cools the earth and nourishes life; to remind you of me. How much I love you could never be answered! All I need is a chance and I will show you HOW MUCH!

In the trenches

I have been there with you, I know your pain as if it were my own; because it is. How can you just give up. There is no way that I can carry you, with all the testimonies we share; victory should be evident. Don't go, we have survived so much together; this too shall pass. Love doesn't die, it may fade but if given the chance and time it can rekindle. We are not done, lets wipe of the mud of these trials and tribulations; begin again and succeed together. Of course there may be more hard times but In the trenches is where true love is built. The heat created by difficulties is the only heat hot enough to melt away this individual—I type way of thinking we are born with. From the heat melting Iron we are forged United as one unit in the image of he. Let us continue this journey together; with a love as strong as ours. We won't be in the trenches for long.

Circumstances

The series of events that led us here, now where do we go. It's like your very voice irritates me. It's not you, it's the way that you carry yourself. You don't listen, yes you hear—but not to understand. You hear for response purposes only. You live to debate about nothing, in your arguments there is no value only innuendo and excuses. I have swallowed my tongue in dealing with you so much that I am now unable to speak. This is draining, you have the aptitude of a child; that refuses to learn. I take my time to explain but you talk during the process and at the end ask questions. You ask questions in seeking answers that if you would just listen during discussions, you would know. I get frustrated yes and suddenly I'm the bad guy. It's like chasing my tail, What on earth is the point? Circumstances lead to decisions, I need to decide!

Who will take time

Who will take time to be by my side when I lose. Who will take time to listen to me when I am of no benefit and have nothing to offer? Who will take time out to be honest with me, not judging but unafraid to be truthful in a friendly way? Who will take time to share with me when I'm down; picking me up and not just step over my body. Who will take time to find me when I'm lost mentally and not heard from. Everyone says that they will be the one but that's hard to believe. Because when times are good most are seen just briefly, so who will be there when times are adverse. Who will take time, to be my friend when I have none? I love me, so I'm more than sufficient alone. But as so many feel comfortable enough to ask the same of me. I just want to know when I'm in need, who will take time?

Friendenemies

Those that pose, acting like they have your back but really don't. We are the best of friends until I leave the room. Once gone you spill all of my tea; everywhere. Then; back in your presence you are my bestie, like I could have no better buddy than you. You wish for me bad, you're not happy when I win. And I'm sure I've seen you crack a smile the times that I've lost. My best friend and my worst enemy all rolled into one. You want to be the brightest out of the two of us, refusing to share the spotlight. Only your accomplishments are regarded. You win we celebrate, I win we ponder your losses. Unfair and I'm unwilling to remain doing this, with a friend like you; who needs enemies. I forgot, friendamie, your both!

Masculine ego patterns

Keep me sometimes trapped inside myself. Unable to see the error in my ways, holding on to a wrong view as to not appear weak. I don't show emotion, not because it isn't felt but due to my ineptness to deal with my feelings. I don't ask for help when I should, totally dismissing your abundant gifts and talents. I am too abrasive at times, giving in to anger and an attitude not in anyway deserving of sharing space—with you. I stumble, I fail but I cover it all up to appear strong. And often times to appear stronger than I truly am. My reasoning behind such ignorance is based upon the soundness of pride. I ask to be able to shake this accursed way of thinking, this stupidity called manhood. Let me think freely with an open mind to escape my Masculine Ego Patterns.

Our first anniversary

This is Our First Anniversary, a day that we will forever share. For this is the day that our United heart print was pressed upon the sidewalk of the universe; for all time and for all to see. I was this day here made complete. Your presence facilitating a union between souls formed eons ago; coming into fruition the day we wed! I am thankful to share this day, Our First Anniversary, the first of many more to come. You are the best decision that I ever could have made, that day I was blessed to be thinking straight. I will honor you all of our days, but let this day mark; Our First Anniversary.

How have you been

You have been on my mind lately, while I do not love you as a lover. You will forever have my heart as a friend. How have you been? I earnestly pray and hope the best for you. In my mind I send to you good thoughts. I have often missed our conversations about life. Your views always interesting and real. I hold no grudges; your past transgressions are just that-past transgressions. Besides, things are meant to teach, not torture. But that is a truth to be accepted by each individual. I know that your excelling, a mind such as yours can't be held back. I reach out to send well wishes rightly deserved from one friend to another. I hope you have learned and allowed your education to bring you happiness. Let faith be the lamp that leads you to your truth. The cosmos is your backyard, explore and attempt to reach its limits. I miss you much and was just wondering. How have you been?

Your secrets are safe with me

I will be there, I promise to love you at your worst. You can open up your heart to me, I will listen. Your secrets are safe with me. I will be your confidant, I am here. You will never regret this choice, my ear is your treasure chest. Fill it with all the wealth that it can hold, and over the years; not a jewel will get misplaced. Your secrets are safe with me, your friend and companion; by your side always. I will protect your heart, by understanding and not judging you. My only action will be to turn my head so that you can fill my other ear with treasure. I am here for you my love, your secrets are safe with me.

I hope

To have you sometime in my future. I know that things don't always go as planned. Mistakes can get in the way of what otherwise would have been good intentions. As Excuses are not meant for human consumption; I will not attempt to feed you any. I will love you from afar for now, but I hope that I will be able to get closer someday. Real love doesn't die, it can fade but it will always live. It beats strong in me for you and I know how you feel. Your anger will dissipate, and my stupidity will one day be forgotten. Then it will be up to the feelings of love inside your heart for me to fight to be heard again. I hope that in time I can hold you and say how happy I am that they were; that you listened to your heart and came home. I hope, that you hope one day you will; too.

This Time

I'm going to treat love different. This time, I promise to respect you. I promise that this time I won't take you for granted. This time I will listen and respond only always in honesty. This time I'm going to be a friend, I'm going to put you first and protect your heart. This time I'm going to incorporate you in my life and stop living separate. I will keep your presence near me like the air that surrounds us all. This time I'm going to amaze and delight you with my level of understanding. This Time I will make you understand that I understand. This time there will be no other times!

There is joy in my heart

So it is easy for me to smile and greet another. Whatever size, shape or color, I can now receive you with open arms. There is joy in my heart so the darkness is gone! Upon its dissipation I was left feeling love. Less judge mental and more accepting. Less careless with my words and more positive. I began being able to care because there is joy in my heart. Now finding that the more I care, the more I care. Exploring myself as I explore these feelings of happiness because there are some I've never felt before. There is joy in my heart and the feeling there, of completeness and power, feels amazing. I speak, I talk and I share because there is joy in my heart.

Capable

You are more than capable of loving me, you just choose not to. We all fight for what we want, well those of us who are blessed with resolve. But who amongst us stays fighting a losing battle? Persistence and quitting; there is a very thin line between the two. Who knows when too little is not enough and when enough is too little? You are capable of telling me the difference between the two, you just choose not to. I'm a victim of wanting to live a life with no regrets, upon dying being able to say in all attempted that I did my very best; that I always hung in there. That I didn't give up early or fight too long in any one battle. Loving you seems to be my cross roads. You won't take me there and you refuse to define what here is. As I await your decision, wait-wait a minute. Has your decision always been made? It seems that I was the capable one, incapable of making a choice! Your choice was made long ago for you, it was me who was inept to your thoughts. It is I who must be capable for me, because you have always been more than capable for you! Decisions made by us all; to prove how truly CAPABLE we really are!

Please pick up

I know your gone, but I still call. In the back of my mind hoping that this is all somehow a bad dream. I would do and give anything just to hear your voice one more time. I wish I could have been there. I would have protected you, you would have come home that night! I know that you're gone, but I still call. In the back of my mind hoping that this is all somehow a bad dream. Missing your presence just doesn't seem right. Your supposed to be here. I sit on the couch waiting for you to walk through the door at night. But you don't anymore, I pick up the phone sometimes and pause before I dial. The feeling becoming ever more real that your gone. I pick up the receiver and instinctively press your numbers. How I wish that one more time you would just please pick up.

You make me so proud

The pride in yourself and the determination you possess at such a young age. I know life appears to be a struggle but you have star qualities, you will surely be a success. I can see that fire in your eyes, you have the fire inside that it takes to make it. You make me so proud, your attitude is authentic. There is no yes in you, all coarseness, all grit. Pure and raw strength, with a magnetic Will. Yes you make me proud, grow and maneuver freely. The only chains designed to hold you back will be those you place on yourself. You are Great, you are a Master and You Make Me So Proud!

The beautiful ones

Beauty is only skin deep, superficial traits will fade and pass like the hours in a day. The gorgeousness under the skin is what I here and now am taking the time out to honor. Your exterior presence my dear may not bring the whistles and calls courted by others, but on the inside where it counts and can never wrinkle or dissipate; you have won countless awards. Your spirit defines what real loveliness really is. Your gentle way and caring manner, have helped men to build empires. Your strong backbone and dedicated Will have shown me what Mrs. America uses to win the crown is worth nothing at all. Your beauty is ageless and transcends time, I know that there is a special place in Heaven for The Beautiful Ones.

I wish you well

In whatever you do, in all your efforts and goals. May the sun always shine on you face and make you feel worthy. Worthy as you are, worthy as your accomplishments make you feel. But more regal than even that, for if all doesn't evolve as you wish; in the midst of lows let the feelings of boundless power surge through your veins. I wish you well, I wish you friendship, I wish for you that which I want for myself! All wisdom, all power, all health, wealth and understanding. I pray that you find and know true peace. Grow and prosper, further life and your experience through love and the attainment of knowledge. I wish you well!